BRITISH AMERICAN RACING

FROM DREAM TO REALITY

PHOTOGRAPHY
GIANNI GIANSANTI

TEXT
GERALD DONALDSON

FROM DREAM

ART DIRECTOR
ROBERTO BETTONI

MANAGING EDITOR **Patrizia Spinelli,**
Edelman Public Relations Worldwide
EXECUTIVE PRODUCER **Gianni Giansanti**

PUBLISHER **Richard Poulter**
PRODUCTION MANAGER **Steven Palmer**
PUBLISHING DEVELOPMENT MANAGER **Simon Maurice**
BUSINESS DEVELOPMENT MANAGER **Simon Sanderson**
SALES PROMOTION **Clare Kristensen**
PRODUCTION ASSISTANT **Imogen Dalley**

COLOUR REPRODUCTIONS **Barrett Berkeley Ltd London UK**
PRINTING **Amadeus Industria Poligrafica Europea**

This first edition published in 1999 by
Hazleton Publishing Ltd, 3 Richmond Hill, Richmond, Surrey TW10 6RE

ISBN: 1-874557-59-4

TO REALITY

We would like to
thank
everyone at
**British
American
Racing**
for their help
with this book,
including
those
not photographed
or mentioned
in the text.

DISTRIBUTORS

UNITED KINGDOM
Biblios Ltd
Star Road, Partridge Green
West Sussex RH13 8LD
Telephone: 01403 710971 Fax: 01403 711143

NORTH AMERICA
Motorbooks International
PO Box 1, 729 Prospect Ave., Osceola, Wisconsin 54020, USA
Telephone: (1) 715 294 3345 Fax: (1) 715 294 4448

NEW ZEALAND
David Bateman Ltd
P.O. Box 100-242
North Shore Mail Centre
Auckland 1330
Telephone: (9) 415 7664 Fax: (9) 415 8892

CONTENTS

"Craig
and I go back a long time.
He's gone from teacher to manager to
'boss', but most importantly we have built up a
strong friendship and have great respect for each
other. Craig is a dreamer, but makes sure his dreams
come true, and any project he gets involved in has to be
taken seriously. Being involved with Craig on this project was
always going to be exciting.

A lot of people questioned my decision to be part of British
American Racing, but the challenge and the excitement of a
new 'big' team entering F1, not only to participate, but to
fight to win, weighed a lot in my decision.

Being part of the building process and
being surrounded by people I
respected

and wanted to work with were other reasons for joining the team. People like Jock Clear, my engineer from Williams, and the mechanics, Malcolm Oastler, our technical director whom I worked with while racing in IndyCars, and Erwin Göllner, my physio/trainer, also from Williams, made it feel like a family.

This season has been a lot tougher than anyone expected, but nobody ever gave up. Race after race, the whole team always fought back, regardless of the tremendous pressure on all fronts, which proves how important chemistry is.

It's a young team where everyone is hungry, everyone is a fighter, where new ideas are accepted and encouraged. It is probably the only team where a development driver – Patrick Lemarie – is there to work for the team, and not there just to be tested himself. This is a driver whose work we can trust, in a team willing to take risks.

Although the results have been way below expectations, I am very impressed with the way the team has worked and gelled. We are very strong and this year's hard-learned experience will pay off massively next year and for years to come. Our spirits are as high as ever and we can't wait to get back into battle and win.

Thanks to all the members of the team who worked unlimited hours. This will have been the hardest. We survived it. Next year's coming and we'll be ready."

JACQUES VILLENEUVE

BRAC

The futuristic architecture of the British American Racing team's new operations centre at Brackley is fronted by an ornamental pond, in which a fountain splashes decoratively. Bordering the pond is a neatly landscaped rock garden, above which three flags flutter in the Northamptonshire breeze. Within the operations centre are the people – the team's heart and soul – whose lives are devoted to British American Racing's millennium mission: to succeed at the pinnacle of motorsport. The team made its Formula One World Championship debut in 1999 and sped toward 2000. . .

life at the operations centre....

speeding into the millennium — ambition, com

ARCHITECTURE IS A BLEND OF ART AND SCI-ENCE. So is the sport in which British American Racing competes and for which its operations centre at Brackley was created. A building is only as strong as its foundation. A Formula One World Championship contender is only as strong as its people. The operations centre focuses the collective strengths of the personnel whose lives are devoted to British American Racing's millennium mission: to succeed at the pinnacle of motorsport.

"I think this is by far the best working environment in motorsport anywhere in the world," says Ron Meadows, now Factory Manager of the headquarters he helped create in a remarkably short time. For 11 months during 1998, Ron took on the role of site manager, as 250 tonnes of reinforcing steel, 1,610 square metres of glass and 120,000 metres of cable and wire were used to transform a green field into this 12,550 square metre state-of-the-art facility.

"We are very well looked after here," Ron says. "Anything anyone on the workforce needs is addressed. There is definitely a feeling of everyone pulling together to make things even better, and that is reflected throughout the building, from the cleaners to the caterers and the people on the shop floor."

Anchoring the operations centre, rising above the angular proportions of the main building, are two semi-circular satellite structures. The tallest of these glass-walled towers, the office quadrant, has four levels. In the top section, senior management personnel are on duty all hours of the day and night. Like the officers on the bridge of a ship at sea, they chart the team's progress, guide it through sometimes stormy waters, mastermind its future, control its destiny.

However, the office is no isolated ivory tower for Chairman Craig Pollock, whose idea the team was and whose ideals it embodies. To help make his vision a reality, to impart it to those who work for him, he uses mental pictures. And when Craig visualises the many departments in the operations centre, he sees the people who make it work.

Across the hallway from his office, Craig Pollock can see a key individual whose contribution to the team includes helping to organise it and then run it. As Craig puts it succinctly, "It would have been impossible to build up British American Racing without Rick Gorne."

Team founder and builder, Commercial Director, Race Operations VP/Director — Rick Gorne's evolving roles are testimony to his many talents. A winning racing driver who became a boardroom success, Rick helped devise the team's commercial and business strategy and, vitally in its formative stages, he was in charge of human resources.

"To set up a new organisation in just a few months," Rick observes, "from a green field site with no staff to a completely equipped factory with a full complement of personnel, was a tremendous challenge. From day one, the biggest challenge was to get all these people working together as a team. Our business is racing, but above all it's a people business.

"People are our most important asset. Starting this facility with a clean sheet of paper, we concentrated on enhancing the working environment for our staff, including such areas as the gym and the canteen. When you walk around the place, you have a sense of it being a very pleasant building to work in."

Another level of the office quadrant contains the legal, commercial, accounting and financial departments, all-important in a sport where fortunes must be generated and spent wisely for ambitious objectives to be achieved.

Tom Moser, Head of Global Sponsorships for British American Tobacco and one of those most instrumental in setting up British American Racing, spent several months in 1999 running the team's commercial department. British American Tobacco, principal shareholder in the team, has about 120,000 employees working in 180 operating companies around the world. In such a large organisation, the contributions of individuals are not always immediately critical to success. This, as Tom notes, is not the case in the relentlessly competitive endeavour British American Racing has chosen to compete.

"In Formula One, the variable for non-performance is zero and the key is getting everyone here to believe in what they are doing and work perfectly together at exactly the same time. This is a terrific challenge and the only variable is the people. There is tremendous pressure to succeed and everybody feels it. There is a great deal of human effort and emotion involved, and from that human investment our team's culture will emerge."

As Commercial Manager for British American Racing, Paul Jordan's duties include ensuring that British American Tobacco gets value for its investment. With an extensive background in racing, covering both the mechanical and sponsorship sides, Paul knows the worth of the many cogs in the wheel that make a up a team that works.

"It's not just one person," Paul stresses. "Everyone from the cleaner to the Chairman plays an important part. What we have created here is very special, and you can see it in this building. Part of my job is looking for commercial partners. When you bring a prospective partner here, you don't have to give them a hard sell. The facility speaks volumes."

In the spacious reception area on the ground level of the office quadrant, the two fully-fledged racing cars on display are sleek and purposeful reminders that the operations centre is also an automotive manufacturing facility.

Behind the circular reception desk, answering the constantly ringing telephones and greeting a steady procession of visitors, are three unfailingly polite and ever-smiling women. They are the public representatives of the human side of a growing organisation that will eventually comprise 300 people.

"We like to create a warm, friendly atmosphere," says Head Receptionist Donna Skipworth-Michell. "All visitors are treated the same, from businessmen to workmen, so that they feel welcome and have an enjoyable experience. It is such an exciting place to work, with so many different things going on."

Everywhere in the building are examples of the fine balance that has been struck between form and function, the need to provide a productive working environment while maintaining a comfortable ambience for the employees.

Ian Costello, who worked on the installation of the heating and ventilating system during the construction phase, became so enamoured with the project that he left his job of 21 years to become the operations centre's Maintenance Manager.

"This is not a conventional facility by any means," says Ian, who looks after everything from waste management to the gardening and the ornamental pond. "It's got much more than you would expect from a standard building because it contains an office environment and a workshop environment under one roof. Everything here revolves around the business of racing. It's very fast-track, and decisions are made instantly with results expected very quickly. It's go, go, go all the time."

On the level beneath the reception area, a fully-equipped fitness centre contains the very latest machines, each of them accessed by an electronic key-card system that automatically programmes a workout according to the specific requirements of individuals.

Next door to the fitness centre are the men's and women's locker rooms, where the employees start and finish their working day. Adjacent to the locker rooms is the lower ground floor of the second satellite tower, which houses the restaurant and the auditorium. From the restaurant kitchen, employees are served breakfast, lunch and afternoon tea. Café-style seating is provided on the main floor, as well as at tables on an upper mezzanine level.

Catering Manager Steve Gray, who also looks after the team's food at tests and races, presides over the restaurant where Wayne Smith is the Chef Manager. At mealtimes, their customers, up to 130 people at a sitting, are served Indian, Chinese, French, Italian and classic British cuisine.

"Our menus change daily," notes Wayne, who formerly worked in hotels and restaurants. "Everything is delivered fresh by 6am, when we start cooking for lunch. A successful day for me is when everyone has enjoyed the food and leaves here happy."

Steve Gray: "Our brief was to offer imaginative menus using the freshest ingredients and to deliver the food with the highest-quality service. Everything has got to be the best, and we always try to improve. How can we get even better? That's the buzz of coming to work every day."

The restaurant's mezzanine level is connected to the auditorium, where an audio/visual system is used to make presentations to team partners. The auditorium is also the location for regular staff meetings and post-race debriefs to keep everyone up to date on the team's progress. It was here, in mid-1999, that Craig Pollock wept with emotion while making the momentous announcement that Honda would become the team's engine partner as the team entered the millennium.

Unfolding behind the twin satellite towers is the main facility of the operations centre. Built on two levels, it is devoted to the design, construction and maintenance of the racing cars upon which British American Racing's fortunes ride.

On the upper level is the design office, where

some 120 technical wizards combine creative thinking with the latest technology to produce blueprints for racing success. The open-plan office space, divided into 3.85 metre square modular work stations seating four people and separated by desk-level partitions, is organised to encourage the flow of ideas among the design specialists, who labour here 12 to 14 hours a day.

Behind the batteries of flickering computer monitors, using advanced computer-aided design (CAD) software, are the designers, race engineers, data engineers, software engineers, buyers and machine tool programmers who create the drawings and crunch the numbers necessary to produce the approximately 3,000 components that comprise the chassis of a Formula One car.

The complete British American Racing chassis is created here on screen, and no one is more intimately acquainted with it than Malcolm Oastler, the Technical Director.

Formerly Chief Designer, Malcolm assumed his new position mid-season, 1999, when his mentor, Adrian Reynard, another of British American Racing's founding members, moved from Technical Director to company Vice-Chairman. Malcolm, who began designing championship-winning Reynard cars in 1987, no longer works alone at his drawing board.

"The complexity of a modern Formula One car," Malcolm emphasises, "means the design process simply cannot be handled by one person alone. Our car is the collective work of the whole technical team. When we set up this department, we were looking for people with a practical background and good analytical ability, who were interested in working as

part of a team in a good environment. We have a group that combines the wisdom of experienced engineers with the energy and enthusiasm of young newcomers. It makes for a great mix."

Just down the corridor from the design office is the human resources department, where Emma Blair works as a Human Resources Officer. Emma, the 50th employee hired, helped recruit many of those who followed.

"Technically," Emma says of prospective employees, "they have to be the highest calibre we can find. We are very conscious of being fair and giving equal opportunities. Personal attributes come into it. You have to be able to communicate, to listen, to work in teams, to be able to add value. You must be enthusiastic, energetic and committed. When you work here, it's not just a job. It is a career. It is your life."

Beneath the design office, the labyrinthian arrangement of departments on the ground floor is designed to facilitate the flow of activities that begin with raw materials coming in at one end of the building, and finish with fully-formed racing cars leaving the other.

In the machine shop, by means of ultra-sophisticated, computer-numerically-controlled (CNC) machines, metals such as titanium, tungsten, magnesium and aluminium are cut, welded, rolled, turned, folded and ground into metallic masterpieces. From a block of solid metal, the machine shop turns out such intricate items as gears for the gearbox and tiny pipe connectors for the car's brake assembly, all produced with incredible precision. The accuracy of these components is measurable to two microns. There are 2,000 microns in one millimetre. If a human hair was split into 75 separate strands, a single strand would be about one micron wide.

Working to such exacting tolerances is a real pleasure for Machinist/Programmer Bob Blanchard, who operates a CNC lathe. After serving as a machinist in the aerospace industry, Bob spent eight years with another Formula One team, located in the south of England.

"It was a big decision to move here," Bob remembers, "because we were well settled where we were. With two young boys, it wasn't easy for my wife and I to relocate. But we came up here, had a look around the lovely area and ended up buying a house in Brackley.

"A main reason for moving was the superb facilities. This is definitely the best factory in Formula One, and we are really well looked after. And my boys are happy because they're heavily into cricket and they're both playing for the Northamptonshire County squad."

Next door to the machine shop is the fabrication shop, where intricate parts such as suspension uprights, radiators and air coolers are cut, welded, bent, shaped and assembled. Much of the fabrication is done by hand, by skilled artisans whose lengthy labours result in finished products that resemble pieces of exotic sculpture worthy of display in an art gallery.

A large portion of the manufacturing area is given over to the various composite rooms, where the complex processes involved in producing the carbon fibre components, which make up about 80 per cent of each car's chassis, are made.

Presiding over the 18 people in the composites department is Sean Gutteridge, who brings 15 years' experience in the aerospace industry to his role of Composites Manager.

"Compared to aerospace," Sean says, "the big difference here is the drastically reduced time frame. And in most instances, the customer is more demanding. I see the race team as my customer, and it is very important to give them an exact delivery date. I am also the supplier, as I see it, to the drawing office. Liaising with the drawing office, trying to design components for manufacture, is a major part of the job."

The people in composites love to talk about the remarkable properties of the material they work with. Five times lighter than steel, but twice as strong, carbon fibre is made by heating and stretching acrylic fibres that are woven into a fabric and impregnated with an epoxy resin. The sheets of carbon fibre, supplied by an outside manufacturer, are kept frozen until needed to prevent pre-curing.

The journey from sheets of raw carbon fibre to finished component begins in the composite clean room, which is kept meticulously clean and completely dust-free. Here, the composite experts weave and trim the pliable sheets and place them in staggered layers over moulds that are made in the machine and fabrication shops. For components requiring extra strength, carbon fibre is sandwiched with aluminium honeycomb in the honeycomb preparation room.

The laid-up mould is then taken to the bagging room, which has an air lock to keep out dust particles. There, it is sealed in a vacuum bag and taken to the autoclave area. In the autoclaves — two large computer-controlled ovens — the component is baked at a temperature of up to 180 degrees C for as long as eight hours.

Nicola 'Nikki' Carrick, a Laminator/Trimmer and the only woman in the composite department, worked for ten years with other teams before joining British American Racing.

"I was drawn here by the atmosphere," Nikki notes, "where everyone has a really strong will to do well. It comes down from Craig, who is so determined to succeed, whereas some other teams seem to be just taking part and are happy to make up the numbers. I felt stale and wanted to work with people who have ambition and determination."

Introduced to the sport by her father, who still competes on motorcycles, Nikki is a racing enthusiast. On the walls at her home, within walking distance of the operations centre, are pictures of the cars Nikki has worked on, often for many hours.

Nikki: "We work very hard here, and sometimes it gets to you. I work with a good bunch of guys and we laugh and joke together. But I do get a bit carried away with my job and can get a bit stressed. Working out in the gym helps, and I do that often at the end of the day. But what makes all this worthwhile is on race days, when you see the car out on the track. You get a real buzz from that, and it reminds you of why you do what you do."

Before Nikki can get her buzz, the composite process must continue. Once it has cured and cooled, the carbon fibre component is taken to the trim room, where it is de-moulded and trimmed, before being bonded to other parts, if necessary, in the composite bonding room. Finally, it is taken to the inspection room. Every component, including those from the machine and fabrication shops, is rigorously checked for the tiniest imperfection before it is taken to the stores department, where it is kept until required for assembly.

Chris Edgell, Stores Section Leader, takes a shopkeeper's approach to dispensing the thousands of parts he and his three colleagues have laid out on their shelves.

"We have a counter at a hatch with a large roller shutter," Chris explains. "We open it up first thing in the morning and close it at the end of the day. You come in and ask for what you want — anything from a tiny washer to an exhaust system for the car — and we give it to you. The only difference is you don't have to pay for it."

Somebody does have to pay for it, however, and that's where Otmar Szafnauer comes in, although his responsibilities extend far beyond cost control. Chief of Technical Operations, Otmar takes over where Malcolm Oastler leaves off.

"My responsibility is making the parts Malcolm and his team design, looking after the manufacture, the quality control, the timing of delivery to the race team and making sure the parts are not too expensive," says Otmar.

In pursuit of the quality that Otmar Szafnauer stresses, the components are taken to the materials and fatigue testing laboratories, located in the research and development department. Adjacent to the laboratories, simulation rigs subject components to all manner of stresses and strains. On the seven-post shaker rig, a complete car, with a life-like dummy representing the driver, is put through its paces on computer-simulated configurations of every Grand Prix circuit.

For perfecting aerodynamic performance, the team uses a full-size wind tunnel, one of the last sections of the operations centre to be built, and one of very few such structures on site at any team's headquarters. Aerodynamic concepts for a car's bodywork are first studied on scale models, then on full-size chassis, with many hours of running in the wind required before the ideal aerodynamic solution is found.

Elsewhere in the manufacturing area, the electronics department deals with such complexities as the wiring harness – linking the sensors, actuators and control units to the car's engine, gearbox, throttle, clutch, differential and so on – that in each car is approximately 1,000 metres long. Here, too, the race team's radio headsets and communications equipment are developed and maintained.

Located along one length of the shop floor is another row of rooms devoted to specific purposes. In the crack-test and cleaning rooms, components pass through X-ray and ultrasonic cleaning procedures. Next door to the gearbox room are the sub-assembly, brake and clutch, and hydraulic departments.

John Digby, whose job title is Hydraulics and Gearbox Section Leader, is nicknamed 'Digger'.

"When riding motocross bikes," Digger explains, "I used to have the odd habit of going over the han-dlebars and on to my head, digging up the dirt with the peak of my helmet."

These days, Digger no longer falls off the bikes he still rides in enduro events, and his head is filled with visions of whirling gears and hydraulic actuators in racing machines. Always fascinated by the inner workings of vehicles, his past experience includes producing hydraulic components for Harrier 'jump jets' and gearboxes for armoured vehicles. Since shifting his attention to Formula One cars, in 1985, Digger has seen gearboxes progress from bulky, manually-operated devices to the tiny, complex, hydraulically-activated, semi-automatic, sequential, six-speed wonders that effect gear changes in milliseconds.

"We are the backroom boys in here," is the way Digger sees it, "while the drivers are the heroes. Jacques Villeneuve can drive the car quicker and his race engineer Jock Clear can get the car to go quicker. We can't. But what we can do, through what we achieve here in the workshop, is give them a reliable car to work with. Gearboxes, and especially hydraulics, can be the Achilles' heel of the car. If we have a failure, I take it personally. I feel as though I have let the whole team down. I investigate the failure and try very hard to make sure it never happens again. Fear of failure can be very stressful, but I love my job."

Next door to Digger Digby's domain is the sub-assembly area, where suspension uprights, steering racks, rocker arms and the like are assembled and serviced. Sub-Assembly Section Leader Jonathan Pain and his group of technicians take great pride in their work, both as individuals and as part of the British American team.

Opposite the sub-assembly, hydraulic and gear-box departments, arranged in one long row, are six race-car bays and one set-up bay. Here, in an environment exactly duplicating the garages at the Grand Prix circuits, the finished cars are assembled and maintained. The portable tool cabinets, manufactured in-house and arranged around the partitions separating the bays, are taken to the races. Suspended over the bays are modules containing lighting, power supply and radio communications. Also in the ceiling, a centralised extraction fan system removes exhaust fumes when the engines are fired up.

On the floor of the set-up bay, to provide an accurate database for setting up the car's complex suspension system, is a solid block of granite. Measuring 5 by 3 metres, the block was hewn from a rock in France and shipped to a specialist firm in the UK, where it took four men labouring by hand for three months to polish to perfection what Ron Meadows describes as "probably the flattest piece of rock on earth".

On the mezzanine floor above the race bays, spare carbon fibre body sections – nosecones, wings, sidepods, engine covers and so on – are stored, ready to accompany the cars and the equipment to the tracks for tests and races.

For 'fly-away' races on other continents, the team air freights 18 tonnes of equipment. Up to 90 tonnes are carried to the European races in three giant, purpose-built transporters.

"Everything that doesn't walk out of here has to come through my department," says British American Racing's Transport Manager, Gwilym Mason-Evans. "We send the cars and all the bits and pieces all over the world. There's the logistical side of it, and my role is also to make sure the vehicles are road legal, that we keep within the laws governing drivers' hours, and so on."

Gwilym has always loved trucks – the bigger, the better. As a teenager, he left the family farm in Wales to sign up with the Royal Air Force, where he served for 15 years in the transport section.

"When I watched Formula One racing on TV, I was fascinated by how they got the equipment around the world. I saw those wonderful transporters, trucks that were far more glamorous than anything I had ever driven. When the opportunity came to join a team, it was a chance not to miss, so I bought myself out of the Air Force and went racing. I worked for a few different teams over the years, and then this ideal situation came up. I walked into an empty office here, and my brief was to set up and run the transport department. It's the best job in the world."

British American Racing's corporate colours, which appear on Gwilym's wonderful transporters and most pieces of equipment that come out of the Brackley operations centre, are the work of eight artistic technicians in the paint shop, located a short distance away from the main facility. Here, colours are mixed by computer to reproduce exactly the elaborate graphic identity specified by the team's image consultants.

On a Grand Prix Sunday, the colourful British American Racing cars – watched by a television audience of approximately half a billion people – carry with them the hopes and dreams of the loyal workforce at Brackley.

17

An inspired blend of art and science, the operations centre is an architectural triumph in a pastoral setting. Here, the new team combines 21st-century technology with age-old human virtues to take on the racing world.

●●● "When I think of this facility, I see faces, I see names and I see individuals throughout the factory. When I think about Research and Development, I visualise the people working under the department head, John Dickison. In the drawing office, which I think of as our heart, because everything we need for the car comes out of there, I see Andrew Green and his team at their computers. In my mind's eye, I can see exactly where each department is, where people are sitting and what they are doing."

CRAIG POLLOCK

Donna Skipworth-Michell, Christine Boswell and Julie Connor offer warm greetings to one and all.

pages 20/21
Frozen in a silver moment of time at a team social event, actors provide a rare instance of inactivity at a facility where the dedicated players perform at top speed, all hours of the day and night.

"There is tremendous pressure to succeed and everybody feels it. There is a great deal of human

effort and emotion involved, and from that human investment our team's culture will emerge."

TOM MOSER

Malcolm Oastler has designed successful racing cars since 1987. Nowadays, given the complexities of the modern Formula One car, his design department employs over 120 people.

pages 26/27
In the giant wind tunnel, aerodynamic efficiency is perfected to produce racing machines capable of flying on the ground at awesome speeds.

Martin Pople and David Hennessy drive the team transporters. Martin helped design the 40 tonne, 16 metre-long futuristic vehicles.

Harry Street hoses
down a car's
undertray. Dave
Hopkinson and Neil
Rimmer demonstrate
the lightness of carbon
fibre – five times
lighter than steel, yet
twice as strong.

●●● "At the end of the day, the driver's life can depend on the chassis and

bodywork composites, so we are a very crucial part of the team."

SEAN GUTTERIDGE

In the research and
development
department, cars and
components are
subjected to all
manner of stresses
and strains. On the
seven-post shaker rig,
a car, complete with a
life-like dummy
representing the
driver, is put through
its paces on computer-
simulated
configurations of every
Grand Prix circuit.

pages 32/33
Stuart Woollen, Gary
Woodward, Mig
Brown and Andy
Gillespie wheel a
'patient' down a
corridor as clean as a
hospital. A steady flow
of raw materials
comes in at one end
of the facility, and
fully-formed racing
cars go out the other.

pages 34/35
Up to 80 per cent of
the 3,000 components
in the car's chassis are
made from carbon
fibre, which requires
baking at up to 180
degrees C for as long
as eight hours.
Alasdair Ryder sits at
the computer-
controlled
autoclave/oven.

●●● "The individual motivation comes from the job itself. It's not production-line stuff at all. It demands a degree of skill, and trying to do it right keeps the enthusiasm up. When we started, and were all thrown into the melting pot, everybody kept their heads down and was concentrating on their own little area. Over time, we got to know each other and it became less of a personal issue. We developed the attitude that we are all in this together and backed each other up. We bonded as a group and a sense of team spirit came into it."

JONATHAN PAIN

The bodywork's paint is stripped off and re-applied after every second race. The celestial motif on the front requires thousands of tiny white stars to be applied individually.

Gary Woodward
(left), Steve Farrell,
Malcolm Oastler and
Mig Brown are part of
the team behind the
technology that
transforms carbon
fibre, aluminium,
titanium and
magnesium into a
605kg car (including
the driver) that will
accelerate from 0 to
100kph in less than
two seconds.

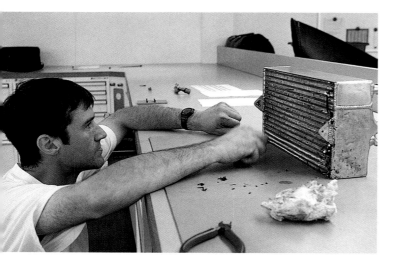

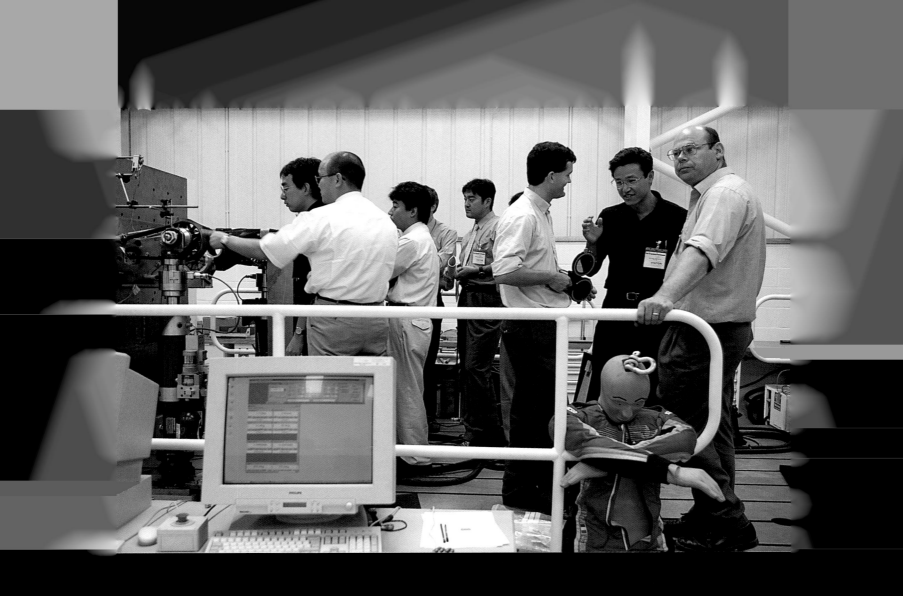

Midway through the
1999 debut season
came the momentous
announcement that
Honda would join
forces with British
American Racing,
beginning in the year
2000. Representatives
from the giant
Japanese auto maker
soon arrived in
Brackley to add their
strength to the team's
millennium mission.

●●● "This is not just an engine supplier agreement – it is a true partnership of co-operation and technology, whereby British American Racing and Honda will jointly develop the chassis. We will make available spaces within our design and development areas for Honda staff. The interchange between Honda engineers and our engineers will stimulate new thought and allow our partnership to develop fruitfully. We are obviously very excited. Honda's great record in racing speaks for itself, and there is a sense of responsibility to want to continue their success with British American Racing."

ADRIAN REYNARD

moments in their life...

A moment is a brief period of time. Formula One competition is all about time. On the track, the point of the exercise is to use as little time as possible. But it takes time to become competitive, which for a new team means an ever growing battle with the constantly ticking clock. For the British American Racing team, the countdown to the millennium was a race against time that left the personnel with precious little time for themselves. Still, there were some memorable moments.

countdown to the millennium – drive, focus,

ONCE UPON A TIME, a little girl used to spend Sunday afternoons with her family watching Formula One racing on TV. Her favourite cars were the red Ferraris and the charismatic French-Canadian Gilles Villeneuve who drove them. She was proud, too, that her mother spelt her nickname, 'Niki,' in the same way as the brave Austrian Niki Lauda. This early interest sparked a passion that would change her life.

Nowadays, Nicole Bearne works for the same racing team as the son of her childhood hero. She thinks Jacques Villeneuve "is a real sweetheart, a lovely guy…it's easy to relax around him. But you can see he is driven, very determined and very single-minded."

Nicole has little time to relax, given the demands of her duties as PA to Craig Pollock. Even on Grand Prix Sundays, when the race team is in action far away from Brackley, times are tense for Nicole. Like most of the personnel who don't travel with the race team, she watches each Grand Prix at home on television. Nicole remembers a certain Sunday in Spain in 1999. There, in only the fifth race of the team's debut season, Jacques Villeneuve's British American Racing entry ran in third position for many laps.

"It was just brilliant!" Nicole recalls. "I was jumping up and down in my lounge, shouting at the television. To see our car, after so many people put so much effort into it, running up there near the front with everybody else trailing behind was just fabulous – until it stopped on lap 40. And then I could have cried."

Dawn Heitman, who works as Rick Gorne's PA, still gets goose bumps whenever she remembers that first indication of the team's real competitiveness. "It was so exciting, so satisfying, to see all the hard work paying off. It seemed so sad for it to end the way it did, but at the end of the day it was very positive because we could see the improvement. What surprised me most was how personally everyone took it, and how we all felt so deeply about our team."

Ron Meadows is based at the factory now, but for nearly two decades he served on the front line with various racing teams, often as team manager. Ron's eldest son Michael – a charter member of the Jacques Villeneuve fan club – races karts, and even when the Meadows family is out at a karting event, they take along a portable television with them to watch British American Racing in action. Ron knows what the team is going through; in fact, he still feels that way himself.

"Up until the start, you're very nervous about what can go wrong. Have the guys put the right amount of fuel in? Have they fastened the bodywork properly? Have they tightened the wheels? What can go wrong this time? You can get completely paranoid. And at the end of the race – win, lose or anything in between – you are absolutely shattered, really worn out."

The sense of urgency inherent in Formula One creates a momentum that is both compelling and nerve-racking. Furthermore, unlike in any other form of business, the bottom line comes and goes very quickly.

"This is not like a business where you wait 12 months for the financial results," explains Robert Synge, the Manager of the race and test teams. "Here, the results come every racing Sunday. It could not be more straightforward, nor could it be more difficult."

Otmar Szafnauer, Chief of Technical Operations, has extensive experience on both sides of the fence in the business of racing.

"It helps to have a racing background," according to Otmar, "but the many people we have here from outside racing, bring experience and diversity that makes us better off. Ultimately, our collective goal is to strive for perfection, to be the best that we can be."

Before he joined British American Racing from the aerospace industry, Sean Gutteridge was a casual follower of Formula One racing, although not necessarily a deeply committed fan.

"I am now," Sean avows. "It is definitely infectious, which is good because it gives more motivation and commitment. I am very oriented towards teamwork, and when we started racing it seemed to bring everyone at the factory closer together. Personally, I get quite upset when we don't do well, which I see as positive because it means I care. I think we all do, and in this business you soon learn to take the rough with the smooth."

The depth of feeling for the team from the people who comprise it, begins at the top. It is said of Formula One racing that the highs are high and the lows are lower than in any other endeavour. Certainly, this has been the experience of Chairman Craig Pollock, right from day one.

"The first high," Craig remembers, "and it was a huge one after negotiating the contracts, was the signing of the documents to begin the joint venture that officially got the team going. That was followed immediately by a serious low, when I wondered, what do I do now?

"The next high came upon signing Jacques, because even though we are very close, I wasn't sure I'd be able to convince him to come to the new team. Moving into the Brackley facility was a fantastic feeling, as was seeing the car going out on the track for the first time. The sense of achievement was immense and our expectations were high."

"Then, as the season started and we weren't producing the results we'd expected, there were some difficult lows to manage. It then became a matter of emotional management to keep up the motivation. To everyone's credit, the motivation to succeed actually increased, and that was a definite plus for the team."

During the low periods there were opportunities for sagging spirits to predominate and debilitate the collective effort. But the team persevered, led by the seasoned veterans who trusted their belief in the old racing adage that suffering setbacks is 'character building'. According to this press-on-regardless philosophy, the resulting strengthened character can power through problems more effectively and come out on the other side a winner.

Rick Gorne's racing career ended in 1979, when – "after a touch of over-exuberance" – he smashed his Formula Atlantic car into an oak tree and broke his legs and wrists. The year before that, Rick was the most successful driver of a Reynard car, winning nine races. Rick, the former racer, then joined Adrian Reynard, who also drove his own cars with some distinction, in a partnership that eventually made their Reynard company the world's most successful manufacturer of single-seater racing cars.

Rick: "After many years in this business, I always expect the unexpected, and when the unexpected comes I'm not surprised. It's not a cynical approach, simply realistic. When we began British American Racing, I knew we were going to have lots of ups and downs, and highs and lows. So I am not deeply disappointed when we have a problem, nor do I get terribly excited when we have success – just a warm feeling of satisfaction. I know from experience that if you keep plugging away and keep up the enthusiasm and the momentum, you eventually get more of those warm feelings of satisfaction."

Rick's fellow team founder, Adrian Reynard, was criticised for being overly ambitious when stating that British American Racing's goal was to win its first Formula One race, an accomplishment that Reynard cars had achieved in every other major category of racing in which they competed.

"Of course, it didn't happen," Adrian acknowledges. "But just to set the record straight, I haven't changed that desire, which has been an implicit part of everything I have ever been involved with.

I still think it is absolutely correct that this team aims to win every race, and I will not be satisfied until that happens.

"I only get satisfied when we win, and then it is only a very temporary satisfaction. If you win on Sunday, you are dissatisfied on Monday. I have been cursed, or perhaps blessed, with being dissatisfied with my own performance all the time. I guess that is what drives me."

"I think you want to concentrate on continuous improvement, so you don't dwell on failure. You learn from failure. What is most rewarding when you look back is the struggle of tackling something new and really difficult. Failing and making mistakes and hurting are all part of the process of building that vital experience. It is not nice when it is happening; it can be very painful. But I would hope in a few years time when I look back, after British American Racing has won world championships, I will derive a level of satisfaction from the fact that we came through in the end. That is what my life – racing life – is all about."

A life in racing came naturally to Jacques Villeneuve. As a little boy, he played in the paddock, pretending to be a famous driver while his father Gilles did the real thing out on the track, until he was killed in his Ferrari in 1982. When he embarked on his own career, under the guidance of his friend and manager Craig Pollock, Jacques quickly made a name for himself.

Rookie of the Year in the Formula Atlantic series in 1993, Rookie of the Year in IndyCar racing in 1994, winner of both the classic Indy 500 race and the IndyCar Championship in 1995, Jacques sped to unprecedented success in North America. The next year, he made his Formula One debut and finished runner-up in the World Drivers' Championship. In 1997, his second season at the pinnacle of motorsport, Jacques Villeneuve won the coveted title that made him the best driver in the world.

In those three formative seasons in North America, Jacques was supported by Player's, a Canadian brand of British American Tobacco, whose Marketing Communications Manager was Tom Moser, like Jacques, a native of Canada. The winning Player's cars were Reynards, supplied by the company led by Adrian Reynard and Rick Gorne.

With this triumvirate, led by Craig Pollock, spearheading the British American Racing venture, Jacques Villeneuve decided to follow.

"There were a lot of unknowns," Jacques admits. "Nobody knew what to expect. We knew it would be risky. The most positive thing was that I worked with these people in the past, and knew the chemistry would be right. There was a lot of work to be done in a short time. It was a big challenge, but that's why you go racing in the first place. You have to believe. You have to dream and then work hard to make it happen."

When it didn't happen immediately and the cars were unreliable, Jacques was forthright about his disappointment. But his belief in the team never wavered, nor did his fierce commitment, which helped inspire British American Racing.

"It was very frustrating not to get the results we wanted right away, not because of what other people might expect, but because of our own expecta-

tions. On the other hand, with a brand-new team any progress you make is an improvement. Every time we improved and made a step forward, the feeling was very positive. We kept motivated because we could always see the light at the end of the tunnel."

"As a driver, you should never stop pushing. You should never stop trying to improve. When you're pushing, you're bound to make mistakes. The important thing is to learn from your mistakes. If you make a mistake, you should avoid making it again, but you shouldn't dwell on it and make yourself miserable. It's the same with a team."

"This team never stopped working very hard. Everyone kept pushing to the maximum, which was great to see. The atmosphere was always good, which showed the real strength of the team. With the troubles we had, it would have been easy for things to fall apart, or for everything to go completely wrong. It didn't. The team stuck together."

"There was never a problem on the human side; it's just that we had a lot of mechanical failures. Most of the problems were with parts we didn't make ourselves, because it took a while before the new factory was able to make everything. Dealing with the mechanical problems, trying to get reliability, meant we had less time to concentrate on getting better performance."

"When you consider that we had to play catch-up a lot of the time, our results were not that bad. The problem is we came in as a big team, with a big factory and a lot of people, so we didn't look like a new team. We were judged as if we were an existing team. The fact is that we were quicker than most first-year teams had ever been."

...CRAIG POLLOCK

Chairman of British American Racing and co-founder of the team, Jacques Villeneuve's manager, successful businessman, sportsman, teacher – Craig Pollock can look back on his considerable achievements with some satisfaction. Instead, he strives for more, pursuing it with unwavering determination and leading by his hard-working example: "Having built up this team with my colleagues gives great satisfaction. There is even greater satisfaction knowing we are going to succeed."

His title is Chairman, but Barbara Pollock's husband seldom has time to sit down. When he does, he's often in transit. So Barbara welcomes an opportunity to accompany Craig on a flight home to Switzerland to see their son Scott.

...JACQUES VILLENEUVE

Contentment in private life is even more precious for those who spend so much time in the public eye. As performers on the world's stage, Jacques and Dannii are known to millions of people, yet being famous can make finding that special someone even more difficult. So, the World Champion driver from Canada and the beautiful Australian celebrity are especially thankful to have discovered each other. Jacques sums up what their relationship means to him: "Love, support, happiness – everything that is really important in life."

Jacques Villeneuve and Dannii Minogue enjoy each other's company in the British American Racing motorhome. Against the odds, a chance meeting between the two famous people at a team function blossomed into a real-life romance.

...RICARDO ZONTA

"This is a very friendly team, like a big family," says Ricardo, for whom family life is very important. When he was only ten years old, his father, a dirt-track racer in Brazil, gave him a kart. Ricardo: "I wanted to be like the Brazilian World Champions Emerson Fittipaldi and Nelson Piquet, and my idol, Ayrton Senna." Twelve years later, after winning championships in every category of racing in which he competed, Ricardo joined the British American Racing "family" at the pinnacle of motorsport.

For Ricardo, being able to jog and work out in a park in his home town of Curitiba, Brazil, meant he was fully recovered from the foot injury he suffered earlier in the season, in his country's Grand Prix.

Commercial Manager Paul Jordan hardly ever stops smiling: "That's because I enjoy my work. You can't really classify it as a normal job, because it has so much diversity. The different people you meet, the different cultures you experience, the challenges you face, the opportunities you are given – what job could give you all this?"

Paul Jordan, temporarily home from his travels, enjoys the good life with his little daughter Daisy.

...PAUL JORDAN

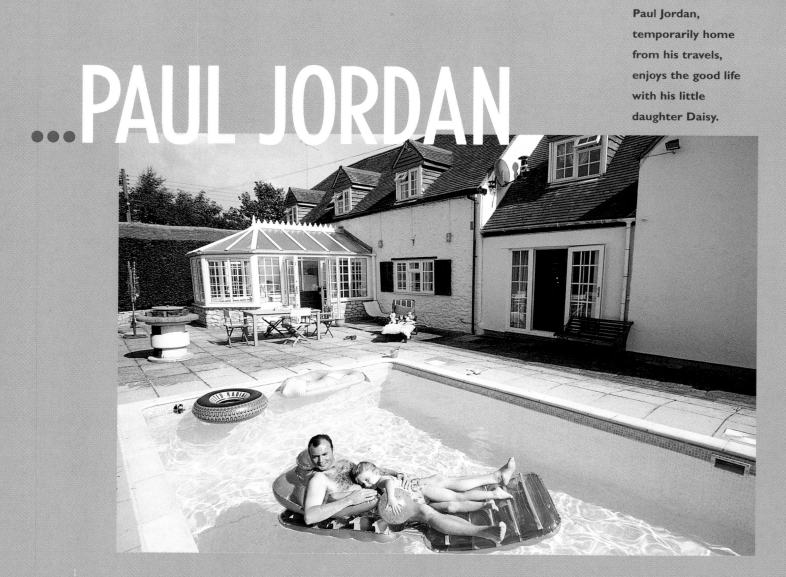

...ROBERT SYNGE

Robert Synge is so
busy racing around
the world with the
team that he seldom
has time to fly himself.

As Team Manager of both the race and test teams, Robert sees yet another airport every few days, although the airfield near Brackley where he keeps his Piper Cherokee is a rare destination. Robert would like to be cleared for take-off more often: "I love flying because it's a great way of clearing the brain and taking your mind off everything else."

...TOM MOSER

"When you have a base to start from, it's easier to move forward," Tom believes. "When you start from zero like us, the way ahead is less clear. Facing a challenge as big as ours, it helps to look back at where we started. When we look back, we can savour how far we've come in such a short time. A British American Racing team that was only a dream has become a reality. When we look ahead, we realise there is much more to do. But what we've done already is a tremendous achievement."

...ADRIAN REYNARD

When recruiting staff for British American Racing, Adrian had about 135 technical positions to fill. There were over 1,000 applicants, many of them attracted by the impressive record of motorsport success associated with the name Reynard. Those hired by Adrian needed specific attributes that would contribute to a collective strength: "And I think I found them, talented individuals with a desire to win, a positive attitude and the ability to become team players and bond into a highly talented group."

He has risen to great heights since designing, building and racing his first car while a schoolboy in 1973. Now he is Dr Adrian Reynard, successful entrepreneur and international businessman, Vice-Chairman of British American Racing and pilot of his own helicopter.

...RICK GORNE

Young Alex Gorne's ancestry suggests he will have an adventurous life. Grandfather Mike was a war hero in the Polish resistance. Alex's dad Rick, formerly a racing driver, was a founding father of British American Racing and is now Race Operations Director.

"In a perfect world, I would like to spend more time with my family. But my wife Marion is used to the racing life by now, and Alex and our daughter Amelia were born into it. We live just outside Oxford, and when I do get home at night the phone never stops ringing. My passion is water skiing. I used to ski every day, but while we were setting up the team I didn't ski at all. To keep the stress levels down, I try and swim every morning and every night. The rest of the time, I'm totally immersed in the business."

...GARY WOODWARD

His MGB restoration project will surely be a winner. After all, Gary Woodward has prepared cars for three World Champion drivers.

Gary 'The Hat' Woodward is the number-one mechanic on Jacques Villeneuve's car. Gary also worked on his car when Jacques became the number-one driver in the world, at Williams in 1997. Before that, Gary helped prepare cars for Champions Alain Prost and Nigel Mansell: "Now I want to help Jacques and the team get to the top in the shortest possible time."

Assistant Team Manager 'Oz' Alsworth rides hard, works harder and knows racing inside out. He spent 15 years working in composites, assembly, fabrication, spares, garage design and travel logistics. Oz used to race motocross bikes: "I loved it in the wet, falling off, getting covered in mud. It's good experience for some Grand Prix weekends."

Andrew Alsworth often rides to work – fast: "It blows the cobwebs away and you scare yourself a bit. It's good fun."

...ANDREW ALSWORTH

... CLAUDIO CORRADINI

"This photo was taken at a team party at Brackley. We were having fun trying to hit as many people as possible, in a friendly way, you understand." As a boy in Italy, 'Chico' Corradini started as a fan of Ferrari and Gilles Villeneuve, then worked for Ferrari for many years. Now, Chico is a Gearbox Technician on Jacques Villeneuve's car.

Claudio Corradini (left) removes wheels during pit stops. Here (with David Lloyd), he tries to do it in a dodgem car.

... SEAN GUTTERIDGE

Sean Gutteridge is a connoisseur of both fine wine and the finely-crafted carbon fibre components produced at Brackley.

"We take a lot of pride in a fine component that looks like a work of art," Sean says of the composite department he manages. "We appreciate that aspect of it, which is also usually a sign of quality. And when you achieve high quality throughout the team, you eventually have the kind of success that you can celebrate with champagne."

...OTMAR SZAFNAUER

As Chief of Technical Operations, Otmar Szafnauer is well-equipped for keeping his eye on the ball.

While playing football at university in his native America, Otmar earned an electrical engineering degree, then a masters degree in business. While serving a 12 year stint with the Ford Motor Company's US racing division, he was also a racing driver, for a team he owned and operated. Formula One is a whole new ball game, but Otmar's goal is unchanged: to succeed.

...RON MEADOWS

After travelling with racing teams for 18 years, as everything from mechanic to manager, Ron was happy to "settle down" at Brackley. So were his wife and three young children. But before he could become Factory Manager, it had to be built. His 11 months as site manager were the most hectic of Ron's career.

Ron Meadows, on the job since the operations centre was only an architect's plan, is especially proud of the new wind tunnel.

...MALCOLM OASTLER

Joanna Oastler awaits husband Malcolm's latest culinary creation. For Australian-born Malcolm, the team's Technical Director, building brilliant banquets on the 'barbie' comes naturally. So does designing successful racing cars.

The Oastlers, with daughters Charlotte and Chloe, try to return to Malcolm's native land at least once a year, usually around the time of the Australian Grand Prix. When he first came to Britain, Malcolm only planned to stay a couple of years on a working holiday. Since his work immediately resulted in winning Reynard racing cars, the designer from Down Under stayed put. Malcolm is justly proud of his cars: "When you watch them run, it's an emotional experience. You're just like an expectant father."

...NICOLE BEARNE

In the fitness centre, Nicole Bearne takes time out from her duties as Personal Assistant to Chairman Craig Pollock.

Nicole spent five years in Moscow, studying, working with British students and as a PA at the British Embassy. She speaks French and German, as well as fluent Russian. A Formula One fan since childhood, she leapt at the chance to come to Brackley. With her Russian husband, who works in assembly, Nicole lives in a small village nearby.

Behind every successful man, it has been said, is an even more successful woman. Dawn Heitman would never make that claim, but her boss Rick Gorne says he couldn't do his job without her. "You never think about being a woman in this team," according to Dawn. "You earn respect from the job you do."

Dawn Heitman, PA to Rick Gorne, also lives in a village near Brackley, with her husband John and their dog Gromit.

...DAWN HEITMAN

71

...JOCK CLEAR

At the races, Jock engineers Jacques Villeneuve's car. Their successful relationship, which began at Williams and resulted in Jacques winning the 1997 driver's title, owes much to their close friendship. Jock, a keen sportsman like Jacques, played rugby at university in Scotland and might have turned professional had racing not taken over his life. Nowadays, he keeps fit by cycling, roller-blading, playing five-a-side football and skiing in winter, often with Jacques.

Senior Race Engineer Jock Clear lives in a converted windmill on a hilltop near Brackley. Jock's whirlwind lifestyle leaves him little time to savour the fantastic view from his home. However, on a clear day, he can see forever.

RAC

life on Grand

CING

Prix weekends...

British American Racing's debut season coincided with a historic occasion on the calendar: a millennium, which occurs only once in a thousand years. Since 1999 was the first year in the team's competition history, every Grand Prix was destined to be a milestone. In eight hectic months of World Championship action, there were 16 races in 14 countries on five continents. The team's memorable journey to the end of the century spanned the globe, and the emotional spectrum.

THE TERM 'GRAND PRIX' COMES FROM THE FRENCH WORDS MEANING 'BIG PRIZE'. Each race for the biggest prize in motorsport, the FIA Formula One World Championship, is called a Grand Prix. In 1999, 11 teams contested the 16 Grand Prix races held around the world. For British American Racing, the newest team, each Grand Prix was an adventure into the great unknown. The competition was fierce, the pace relentless, and by the end of the pressure-packed season, the team had come of age.

On a Grand Prix weekend, the cars practice on Friday, qualify on Saturday and race on Sunday. But by the time the race has been run, the team will have packed a remarkable amount of work into a relatively short period of time. In fact, the work begins well before the main event, when the British American Racing transporters and motorhomes arrive at the circuit.

Charged with the task of driving the three main transporters to the races are six 'truckies', led by Chief Truckie Martin Pople. Over a period of 12 months, Martin helped design and build the 40 tonne, 16 metre long behemoths that go well beyond conventional trucks and are the most technically advanced in the racing world.

When Martin and the truckies drive them on the roads, on journeys that can take up to two days for the circuits furthest away from Brackley, the two main transporters are the regulation height of just over 4 metres. On arrival at the circuit, however, a button is pushed in each of them, and in about three minutes six hydraulic rams raise the roofs to their full height of 5.3 metres.

Martin acknowledges that the transformation of the trucks into comprehensive versions of the operations centre itself is "kind of mind blowing". The race truck carries three race cars and enough spares to make a fourth car; at the track, it becomes a machine shop. The second truck transports the spares and has offices upstairs. The third truck, which contains all the equipment for the garage set-up, is driven by Dave Hennessy and fellow truckie Trevor Bailey, who are the first to arrive at the circuit.

"We get here on the Sunday before the race and start by cleaning the garage floor, then painting it," says Dave, who studied geology in his native New Zealand before embarking on a career in motorsport. He is also responsible for garage presentation, and explains how he and his team mates leave no stone unturned in their quest for the slickest presentation in the paddock.

"On Monday morning, we come in and set up the garage, installing the wall panels, the overhead modules, and so on. It takes us about a day and a half. From then on, with the other truckies, we keep everything spic and span, cleaning and polishing the garage and the trucks for the rest of the weekend. We probably put more effort into presentation than other teams, and they notice it. There is a lot of competition in a Formula One paddock."

When it comes to competition in the motorhome division, Paul Edwards thinks that the team's two units — one for British American Racing and one for its engine supplier, Supertec — are at the top of the league.

Competition comes naturally to Paul, a racer who was British Hillclimb Champion in 1989, then 'chief cook and bottle washer' for several racing teams before he accepted the British American Racing challenge.

"Craig told me the goal was to set the highest possible standards," Paul says of the motorhomes that, at 6.2 metres, are the tallest structures in the paddock. "They're more like buildings. Including the main vehicles, which are raised hydraulically like the transporters, and the awning structures that fit alongside them, with the spiral staircases and all the furniture inside, it takes six of my people 26 man-hours to set each one up."

Paul, and his staff of 32, also look after the team's catering and hospitality, at Brackley and at the races. In addition, he is in charge of transporting senior team personnel and VIP guests to and from the airports and the circuits on Grand Prix weekends.

Making sure the team's commercial partners and VIP guests receive the full Grand Prix experience is part of Commercial Manager Paul Jordan's job. With a racing background that began in 1980, and included stints as a mechanic and team manager, Paul uses his extensive motorsport knowledge to enlighten and entertain guests in the Paddock Club.

"The Paddock Club is always in the best location at each Grand Prix," Paul explains. "The decor of our suite features the British American corporate identity and everything we do — the presentation, the food and wine, the service — is done to the high standards set by the team. On average, we entertain about 50 guests over the weekend. We keep them up to date with the team's activities, take them on visits to the garage and on pit-lane walkabouts, bring the drivers and senior team members to talk to them, and so on. Inevitably, they're surprised and mighty impressed by just how much effort the team puts into a Grand Prix weekend."

Should Paul Jordan want to give the team's guests a quick lesson in the amount of effort required, Race Team Manager Robert Synge speaks eloquently on the subject.

Robert: "Every team in the Formula One paddock does a fantastic job and works massively hard at it. It takes a huge passion for the sport to get the job done. There is enormous pressure to get it done right. In other types of racing, when you make a mistake, few people notice. Here, the whole world is watching and it can be intimidating. The task is daunting, astonishingly difficult. You need masses of enthusiasm and the deepest possible belief in yourself and your team-mates to achieve your ambitions."

Robert Synge's racing ambitions began when he was a student at Stowe, the school near Brackley that also happens to be within earshot of the sounds of Formula One cars howling around the Silverstone circuit.

"I remember the day exactly," Robert recalls.

"Jackie Stewart, three times a World Champion in his career, came down from Silverstone, where he was racing, and gave a 20 minute talk on the front steps of the school. I remember hanging on to his every word and being absolutely captivated. From that day onwards, I knew the only thing I wanted in life was to go racing. I was 12 years old."

Robert went racing, at first as a driver, then eventually as the entrant of championship-winning teams in several categories. Now, to compete against opposition that includes a team fielded by Jackie Stewart, Robert manages a British American Racing team composed of personnel from many different backgrounds, although they share some common characteristics, as he explains.

"They must have the right combination of enthusiasm, dedication, motivation and personality. Assuming they have the appropriate mechanical skill, they don't necessarily need to have had a formal engineering or mechanical education. Practical experience can be invaluable when it comes to dealing with the emergencies you get here on a regular basis. We don't hesitate to bring in new people from outside the sport. With no preconceptions, they assimilate easily, and as newcomers they're less likely to get burnt out and will have a longer career with us. We think we have the ideal blend of experienced and new people."

British American Racing's Assistant Team Manager Andrew 'Oz' Alsworth, in Formula One racing since 1985, knows what it takes to go the distance. "As the season goes on, it does wear you down. You put so much energy into a race weekend, and at the factory, and you can't let up. Sometimes you feel down when the going gets tough, but that's

part of it. You just keep your head down and work, work, work."

The workload is shared by over 40 people on the race team, which is organised and run like a well-drilled army. The military connection is apt for Chief Mechanic Alastair Gibson, whose background includes serving as a corporal in the South African Army during the war in Angola. For Alastair, a born adventurer whose father was a Grand Prix mechanic, a racing career was perhaps inevitable, although sometimes it can be a battle.

"When things aren't running smoothly," according to Alastair, "you have to be able to chew gum and tie your shoelaces at the same time. The pressure is really huge when you have engine changes, gearbox changes, hydraulics problems to solve. You are running around trying to get the right people to fix the right problem."

"For me, the most tension is at the beginning of the weekend, leading up to the first hour of practice on Friday. To that point, you are deeply concerned with making sure the cars are set up according to the engineering specifications. Once they run that first hour, you're going flat out for the rest of the weekend and the pressure is pretty constant."

Constantly on the go is Chief Engineer Steve Farrell, whose duties include working with Technical Director, and fellow Australian, Malcolm Oastler, to determine the specifications for the cars. During his time with the championship-winning Jaguar sports car team, Steve was nicknamed 'Skippy,' after a kangaroo cartoon character. Now he is known as 'Otis' because Alastair Gibson thinks he looks like the musician Otis Redding when he wears sunglasses.

Like Alastair, Otis sees an analogy between racing and war.

Steve Farrell: "My father used to say the best years of his life were in the Second World War, because of the camaraderie that developed among the troops. Going through what is really a bit of a battle here, I think a strong team spirit is developing, rising like a phoenix out of the fire. This is something you can't go out and buy, you have to earn it."

"As I keep saying to people, you have been given the tools to do the job, and if you can look at yourself in the mirror on Monday morning and honestly say you've done the best possible job over the weekend, that's all we can ask of you. It will all come together as a result of that."

On the road with racing teams for 30 years, Steve Farrell never forgets the people back at base. When the team returns to Brackley from a Grand Prix weekend, Steve is one of those who takes part in a post-race debrief.

"I tell them that it's not just the 40 or so guys in the front line at the races. When everybody takes pride in their job, including those at the factory, they are making a contribution in real terms to the whole team effort. For instance, when we're unwrapping a new part for the car, if it's nicely packaged and properly labelled, it adds that little bit more to our efficiency at the track."

At the circuit, looking after approximately 2,000 spare parts, which range from suspension wishbones to the smallest nut on the car, is Spares Co-Ordinator Simon 'Whiplash' Wachter, who works out of a room in the back of one of the team's transporters. Beginning as a truckie in 1988, Whiplash drove from Formula 3 racing into Formula 3000 and arrived at a destination he never thought possible.

"I never imagined it would lead to this," Simon says, "only because it seemed so far beyond my reach when I started. I love this job, absolutely love it, because it has stretched me so far and given me the opportunity to excel. It's taught me that you don't know what you're capable of and that anything is possible when you put your mind to it."

The mind of Ted Bowyer, now concentrated on his job as Electrician on Ricardo Zonta's car, used to be centred on the music business. Ted thinks having organised music festivals and head-banging rock concerts was an appropriate background for working on cars that shriek louder than the 'heaviest' of heavy-metal groups.

"In the music business, I got a lot of experience with crisis management," Ted relates, "and that's useful in the hectic racing environment. Formula One electronics are very complicated, but I know my job inside out. You work hard, sometimes 20 hours a day or more. When everything you've done works perfectly, it means you've played your part in making the car go and you get a real sense of achievement. If something goes wrong, you feel gutted."

Claudio 'Chico' Corradini, born near the Ferrari factory and a veteran of many years as a mechanic with the famous Italian team, before becoming the Gearbox Technician on Jacques Villeneuve's car, is accustomed to the ups and downs of racing.

"Sometimes when results are slow to come, you

79

feel very disappointed and dragged down," admits Claudio. "But the motivation is still there. It might even grow, because you want more than ever to turn things around and be able to smile with your team-mates and say, 'Okay we've done it. We've proved we can do the job, we showed the world we could do it.' But this takes time. You can't build a house starting from the roof. What we are doing is building a strong foundation."

Building up to race day, the team's activities intensify. On Saturday afternoon, beginning immediately after the crucial hour of qualifying, the mechanics rush purposefully around the garage, preparing the cars for the race. In pursuit of reliability, engines, gearboxes, suspension components and most critical moving parts are replaced with newer equipment. While the work in the garage continues apace – for about seven hours non-stop on a normal Saturday afternoon – the engineers are meeting in their transporter office to determine the race set-up for the cars, and also to begin to map out the strategy for the race.

Those taking part in the meeting of engineering minds include Steve Farrell, Race Engineers Jock Clear and Mick Cook – responsible for the Villeneuve and Zonta cars respectively – and their Data Engineers, David 'Pink Floyd' Lloyd and Guillaume 'Rocky' Rocquelin. Jock Clear explains what goes on in the engineering inner sanctum.

"We all share the same office, so ideas are thrown around freely," reveals Jock, whose credentials include a degree in mechanical engineering and the hands-on experience of race-preparing the Williams cars in which Jacques Villeneuve won 11 Grands Prix.

"The drivers sit down with us, tell us what their concerns were during practice or qualifying and what they would like improved for the race. But by then, we have massive amounts of data that have been collected over the two days, and also from test sessions, to point us in the right direction for the race set-up. We don't arrive at our final race strategy until about mid-day on Sunday, after the warm-up, but on Saturday night, we generate the information from which we will make our decision."

At about 10 o'clock on Saturday night, the engineers issue set-up sheets from which the mechanics fine-tune the rebuilt cars. Since the job list for each car contains spaces for 41 separate tasks, ticking them all off can take quite some time, even on an ordinary weekend.

On one extraordinary weekend in Belgium, both Ricardo and Jacques suffered huge accidents in qualifying at the notoriously dangerous Spa circuit. Neither driver was hurt, but the work of salvaging raceworthy cars from the wreckage went on until daylight on Sunday morning. Painful as it was, the labour-intensive experience became a positive force that served to further unite the team.

Craig Pollock: "We started off the season as a group of people who hardly knew each other, and by that Spa weekend it was absolutely clear that the group of people had become a team. When they worked all that Saturday night in the garage, and I was there to see what I could do to help ease their pain, the guys were just brilliant. There wasn't one long face, and that made me really proud of them."

According to Jock Clear, "the morale was always

tremendous considering what we went through, particularly with reliability problems. It surprised me a bit, because I've seen well-established teams get into serious slumps over far fewer frustrations. There was never a time when these British American Racing guys didn't jump out of bed in the morning, if they had any sleep, and say, 'right, today we are going to make a difference.'"

In 1997, while Jock was responsible for engineering the car that Jacques Villeneuve drove to become the World Drivers' Champion, Ricardo Zonta won the Formula 3000 driving title in a car engineered by Mick Cook. When Jacques won his championship, the first person he thanked was his good friend Jock. Ricardo says, "Mick has helped me a lot and he is a good person." Mick Cook's motorsport career began when he was a 15 year old motorcycle racer. After seeing too many riders killed, and being injured himself, he turned to racing on four wheels, at first driving the cars, but then becoming a winning team entrant and race engineer. A successful relationship between race engineer and driver is more than just a mechanical connection, as Mick points out.

"Some people forget the psychological needs of a driver and just treat it like a technical or business exercise. But the driver is the most important part of the human equation in the team, and they sometimes need help coping with the problems and the risks they face. I'm very conscious of that and do what I can to support Ricardo emotionally."

Emotions run the highest on race day, which begins with the warm-up session, a stressful period of time for the team's Race Operations Director Rick Gorne.

"Operationally," Rick explains, "the most anxious time for me is definitely the Sunday morning warm-up, because we have a lot to do and only 30 minutes to do it. We have to get the drivers in and out of the garage, running both race cars and the T-car. Time is of the essence and everything has to run like clockwork."

As the clock ticks inexorably toward the start, the tension mounts progressively. All his years in the sport, in which he began as a racing driver, haven't dimmed the strong emotions that Rick experiences during those nerve-racking moments leading up to the start.

"At 2 o'clock on Sunday afternoon, I am in the garage watching the TV screens and the timing monitors. I must admit that it gets my heart racing, with a mixture of excitement, anxiety and expectancy."

Hearts are also racing out on the pit wall, where the team's two timing stands are located. Mick Cook, Rocky Rocquelin, Otis Farrell and Oz Alsworth watch over Ricardo's car. Concerned with Jacques' car are Jock Clear, Pink Floyd Lloyd, Robert Synge and Craig Pollock.

"I am a lot more nervous than I ever thought I would be on race day," Craig admits. "Just before the start, my heart rate must go up higher than the drivers'. It's not so much fear of accidents, although that is always a worry. My main emotion is not wanting to be disappointed. What I care about most is that the cars will be competitive and reliable so our drivers have the chance to do well for themselves, for the race team and for everyone back at Brackley."

Screaming engines, racing pulses. Men and machines at their limits.

Fierce competition,
relentless pace,
maximum effort at
the pinnacle of
motorsport.

Tension-filled teamwork. Servicing the car with split-second precision.

TALK

NEUTRAL

REV

R

Gripping speed.
Skilled hands, a
concentrated mind,
a brave heart.

Even with his driving shoes undone, Jacques remains the consummate racer.

On the wrong side of
the fence, Jacques is a
reluctant spectator.

starting a world away from Brackley...

Melbourne's Albert Park circuit is about as far away from Brackley as it's possible to go, and the team's first Grand Prix weekend went reasonably well. Unloading three race chassis and 17 tonnes of equipment, setting up the cars for practice, qualifying and racing, planning strategy, starting the race, racing, executing pit stops – everything was done for the first time in competition. After qualifying in midfield, Jacques raced as high as eighth until being forced out by a rear-wing failure. Until stopping with a gearbox problem late in the first Formula One race of his career, Ricardo seemed on course for a points finish in the team's debut.

The world watched as Jock and Craig awaited the start of British American Racing's first Grand Prix. The people in the race team and those back at Brackley viewed it with a mixture of elation and apprehension.

95

No time to lose. From
Australia, the race
team flew back to base
at Brackley. While the
cars were readied for
the next Grand Prix,
testing continued
apace at various
circuits, with Jacques,
Ricardo and the team's
official test driver,
Patrick Lemarie.

••• "You don't have time

to notice the fatigue. You're going flat out all the time, so you only feel tired when you stop."

ALASTAIR GIBSON

For the race team, a Grand Prix weekend starts quickly, then speeds up. The hours are long, the work hard, moments of respite brief and few and far between.

Ricardo's setback at his home Grand Prix...

Ricardo was excited by the prospect of performing in front of his countrymen at Interlagos, a circuit he knows like the back of his hand. Unfortunately, in practice he went off the track and crashed at 170 kph into a steel barrier, suffering a foot injury that would force him to miss the next three races. Shocked by the incident, although relieved that Ricardo would recover fully, the team soldiered on at the Sao Paulo circuit. With his teammate in hospital, Jacques raced courageously on the weekend of his 28th birthday. Relegated to the back of the starting grid due to a fuel discrepancy, he fought his way up through the field to seventh place before retiring with hydraulics problems, three quarters of the way through the race.

David Lloyd is the Data Engineer for Jacques' car. On his telemetry monitor, 'Pink Floyd' Lloyd can see that the level of commitment from his driver is never less than total.

the highs and lows of racing...

A scintillating qualifying lap by Jacques planted his car fifth on the grid and provided the team with the best starting position in its short history. "When going for a quick time," Jacques reveals, "I give myself a pep talk to build up my aggression level. During the quick lap, you have to give everything you have – all the energy and emotion. You're tensed up and not nearly as relaxed as when you're racing." Neither is Craig Pollock, who is fully aware of what goes into a Jacques-attack. "In qualifying, I am a little bit worried about him, because I know Jacques is going to go for the maximum, perhaps more than the car is capable of. Knowing that he is on that razor edge on a quick lap scares me a bit and keeps me on the edge of my seat."

Tense times for Tom, Malcolm, Adrian and Craig as the team's fortunes fluctuate. At Imola, there was euphoria when Jacques qualified fifth, despair when his car stalled on the grid, and finally some satisfaction after the teams first race finish.

108

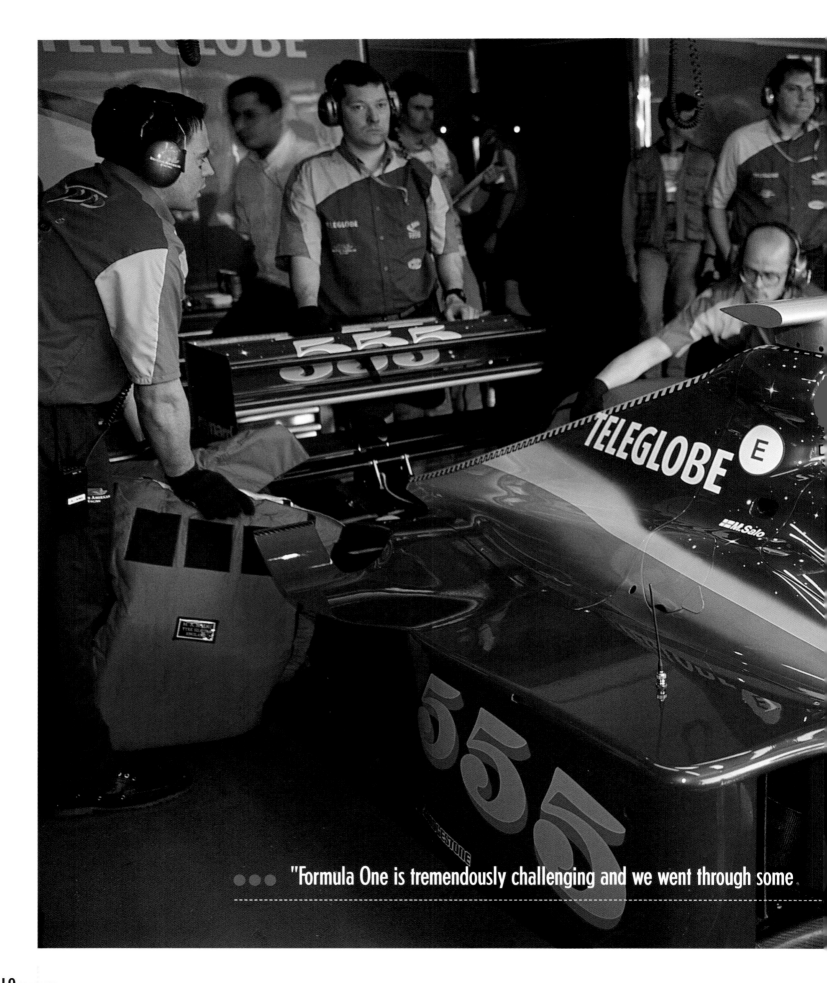

"Formula One is tremendously challenging and we went through some

tough times. But we're at the pinnacle of motorsport, so it should be tough."

STEVE FARRELL

Mika Salo drove in three races while Ricardo recovered from his injury. In the San Marino Grand Prix, a gearbox problem stalled Jacques at the start, but Mika was classified seventh, giving the team its best finish to date.

Over 40 people make up the race team. Their job titles include the Team Manager and his Assistant, a Chief Mechanic, a Chief Engineer, an Electronics Chief and the Team Secretary. Each of the two race cars has a Race Engineer, a Data Engineer, a Number One Mechanic, two Number Two Mechanics, a Hydraulics Technician, a Gearbox Technician, an Electronics Engineer and an Electrician. Three additional Mechanics work on the spare, or T-car. There is also a Spares Co-Ordinator, an Engine Dresser, a Sub-Assembly man, a Radio Engineer, two Composite Repairmen, a Wing Assembly man and six Truckies. Many of these people have other duties on race weekends – 21 of them are members of the pit crew. Some also work on the test team, which has about 25 people performing duties similar to those on the race team.

A job list for the overnight preparation of a car can include over 40 separate tasks to be performed, from changing an engine to fitting the driver's drink bottle.

Waiting for those adrenalin-packed moments when they must change four wheels and add 50 litres of fuel can seem like an eternity for the pit crew. But for many, it is the highlight of the weekend.

●●● "I hold the lollipop which controls the pit stop. At the end of the day, you're responsible for the safety of all those people, so you don't want to lift the lol- lipop and release the car too soon. But you can't lift it a millisecond too late, or time will be wasted."

ALASTAIR GIBSON

performance potential is realised...

In Spain, a superlative start made Jacques a front-runner for the first time. A mechanical failure left him disappointed, but encouraged that the performance was there. Weighing a minimum of 600 kg with the driver on board, the BAR-01 car is 4470 mm long, 1800 mm wide and 950 mm high. Powered by a 3 litre engine weighing about 100 kg and developing close to 800 bhp, the car can reach over 160 kph in first gear, exceed 190 in second, 225 in third, 240 in fourth, 275 in fifth and well over 325 kph in sixth. Cornering at high speeds subjects the driver to forces of gravity of up to 4g, four times his body weight. In slowing the car from speed, the carbon fibre brakes glow red hot at temperatures of over 1,000 degrees centigrade and the driver must withstand up to 5g deceleration.

Jacques can accelerate his BAR-01 from zero to 162 kph in 4.6 seconds, then stop it in 3.1 seconds. It may be a short time on the clock, but it's hard work in the cockpit.

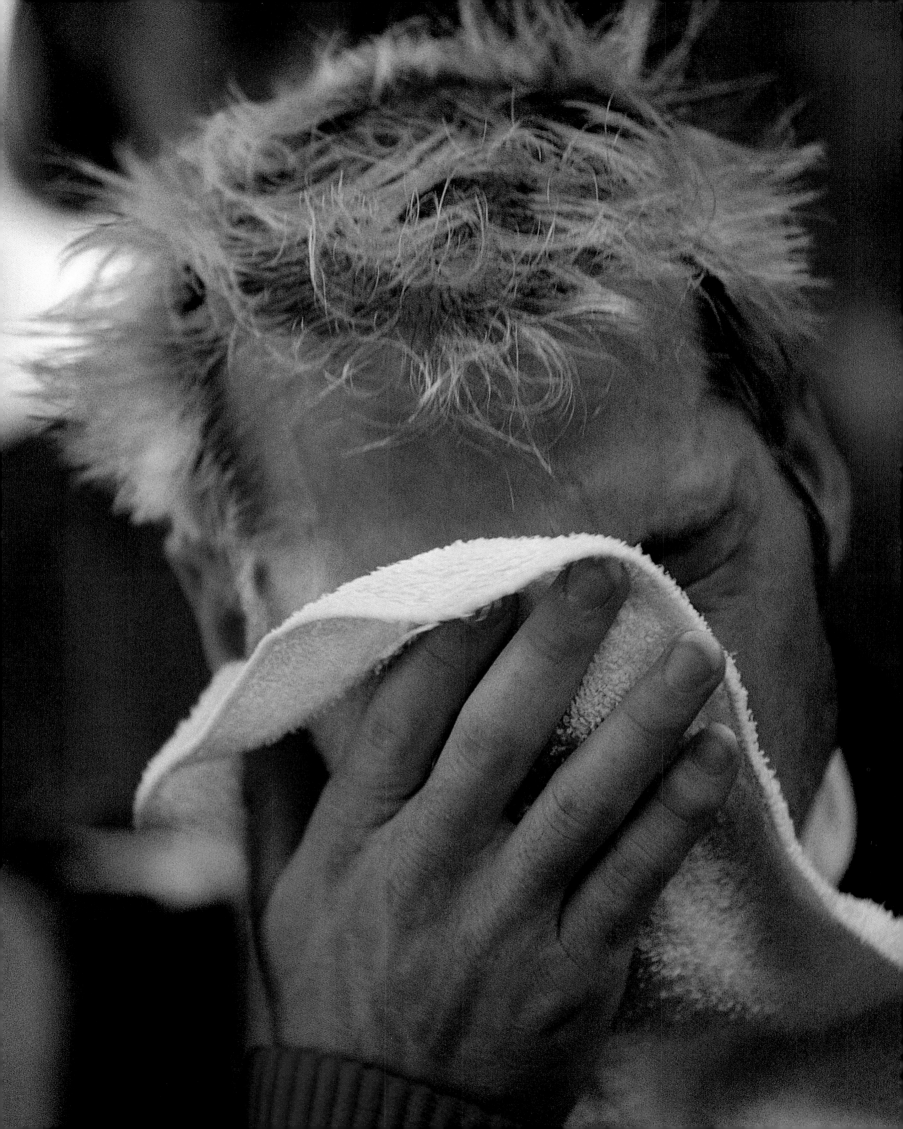

SEX IS BETTER THAN F1
And so many girls
throw themselves at
Jacques *Villeneuve*
that he should know

All work and no play
would make Jacques a
dull boy, which he
most certainly isn't.
Nor is the playful
Dannii, whose
rapport with her man
includes a shared
sense of humour.

● ● ● Jacques enjoys a light
moment in the privacy of the
team's motorhome. The team
takes two motorhomes to the
circuits in Europe. Parked in
the paddock near the garages,
the luxuriously-outfitted, two-
storey units combine office
space for team principals, as
well as kitchen and restaurant
facilities for race personnel
and invited guests.

A few months after it
was first tested at the
Barcelona circuit, a
British American
Racing car ran in
third place in the
Spanish Grand Prix.
In the team's most
competitive showing
to date, Jacques was
able to hold off
Michael Schumacher's
Ferrari for the first
third of the race.

● ● ● "When a bunch of people gel together, you get the chemistry you need to make a team work. Rick [left] I've known since we were racing in North America. Craig [right] I've known for many years. They're both fighters and hard workers. Their personalities fit well, and their positive attitude is taken up by the whole team. It's the same with people like Jock Clear and Gary Woodward. We worked together at Williams and won the Championship. So we know what it takes."

JACQUES VILLENEUVE

When his mind is in racing mode, Jacques prefers to keep his helmet on. He designed the colour scheme himself. It fits well with his driving suit, although the suit is several sizes too large – another Villeneuve trademark.

no luck for the local hero or his fans...

Le Circuit Gilles Villeneuve in Montreal is named after Jacques' late father, whose memorable victory here in 1978 was his first in Formula One. The Villeneuve family home where Jacques spent his childhood is nearby, as is a museum devoted to the spectacular career of the legendary Gilles, who was killed in a tragic racing accident in Belgium in 1982. For Jacques, his home Grand Prix is the most important of the year, and he loves returning to his favourite city. This year, he was welcomed by what he called "an amazing card". The huge greeting card, presented by telecommunications conglomerate Teleglobe, British American Racing's Canadian-based commercial partner, was signed by some 4,000 Villeneuve fans. Alas, their good luck wishes were in vain. "It was my mistake," Jacques admitted after crashing half-way through the race. Ricardo, whose return to action ended similarly, noted that he was in good company, "as three World Champions – Hill, Schumacher and Jacques – all went off at the same place."

Performing in his home Grand Prix, on the circuit named after his father, made Jacques the focus of attention. The local hero gave his fans plenty to cheer about, while he lasted.

From racing around the park in the heart of Melbourne and through the streets of Monaco, the Formula One world tour continued, taking the team to the majestic venue of the cosmopolitan city of Montreal. Beyond lay Magny Cours, Monza, Malaysia and more.

Principals watched
from the timing stands
as the personnel
persevered.

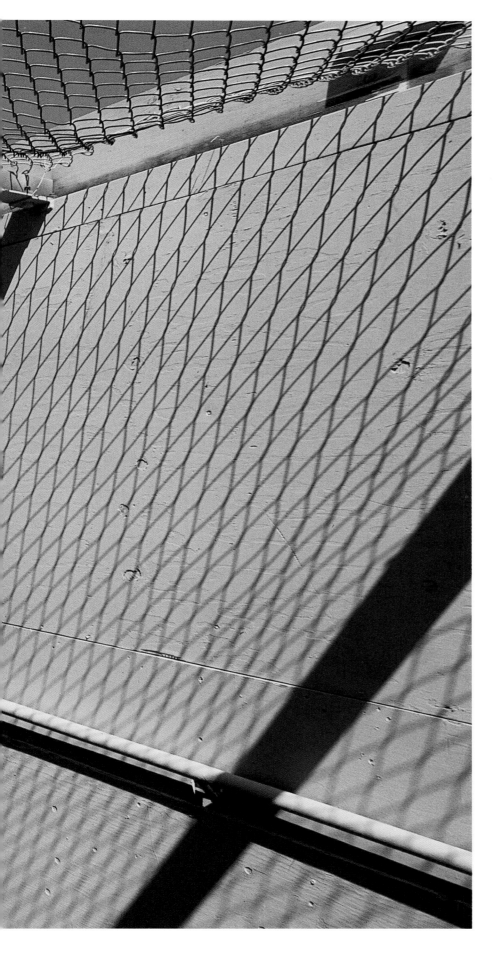

●●● "Ricardo is a great guy. The whole crew gets on really well with him. We have some fun and sometimes get together with him socially. He's laid back, easy to work with, and that makes you want to work harder for him. His injury interrupted his learning curve, but he recovered and came back to have some good races."

BARRY GOUGH

Ricardo and Jacques are heroes around the world, especially for the fans at Il Grande Premio do Brasil and Le Grand Prix du Canada.

finally, a finish for Ricardo...

Ricardo's ninth place in France was his first race finish for the team. Jacques spun out in the atrociously wet conditions, where the pit crew worked overtime changing tyres, which they can do in just over three seconds. Adding 50 litres of fuel takes about five seconds longer. At the left front wheel, Barry Gough operates the airgun, Terry Wasyliw takes the wheel off, and Mig Brown puts it on. Their counterparts at the right front wheel are Paul Johnstone, Derek Noble and Gareth O'Ryan. At the rear wheels are Paul

Bennett, Gareth Williams and Dave Hopkinson, and Gary Woodward, Chico Corradini and Andrew Neale. Richard Moody and Neil Rimmer operate the front and rear jacks. Harry Street is the re-fueller, Stuart Woollen is the hoseman, Peter Arkell stands ready to shut off the fuel flow in an emergency, and several firemen stand by. Ted Bowyer steadies the car, Mark Willis puts a new nosecone on if necessary, and Alastair Gibson – 'Mr. Lollipop' – waves his magic wand to release the car.

Maintaining strict
discipline while
performing 'under fire'
in a pit stop is only the
most dramatic
example of the
extreme pressure the
team faces every
Grand Prix weekend.

a disappointing home Grand Prix...

The team's shortest trip of the season gave many of the factory personnel the opportunity to have a first-hand look at their team-mates in action. The visit to Silverstone was followed on Sunday night by a party at Brackley, where there was much to discuss. Mechanical problems prevented both Jacques and Ricardo from finishing the British Grand Prix, which marked the mid-point in the team's first season. Jacques spoke for everyone when he said, "It's frustrating to finish the first half of the season like this. For sure, we're way behind where we thought we'd be by this stage. But you've got to remember this team is only eight races old. All the hard work we've done so far has not been wasted and we will continue to improve."

Silverstone studies. Rick entertains the mechanics in the garage, Jacques looks for the Gorne show, Oz Alsworth holds the phone and Martin Pople his head.

The two main transporters travel at the regulation height of 4 metres. In the paddock, however, hydraulic rams raise the roof to 5.3 metres, creating two-storey office and workshop areas.

●●● "The concept behind these trucks was to create extra space at the races, where space is always at a premium. We've got what we think is the best factory in racing, and that's what we wanted with the trucks, with working units second to none presented in the best possible way. We used the corporate colours of blue and darker and lighter grey to tie everything together, both inside and out, so there's no mistaking the British American Racing team, on the road and at the races."

MARTIN POPLE

Enthusiastic Formula One fans show their support for the 22 drivers of ten nationalities, who race for the 11 teams, which are based in four countries.

a test of character in the Alps...

In the 71 lap Grosser Preis Von Osterreich, Jacques ran as high as fifth and remained in the top ten for the first half of the race. Ricardo was right behind him, proving that he was back in top form and that the team's cars were again competitive. But they were still fragile. Jacques' race ended on lap 34 with a broken driveshaft, and Ricardo's on lap 63 with a clutch failure. While the mechanical misfortunes took their toll on the track, the team's commitment and resolve to surmount them never wavered. "The most amazing thing," Craig Pollock said, "is how they came through all our frustrations. Even though we started slowly and had poor reliability and few finishes, the team never, ever gave up. We got stronger and stronger."

While cattle grazed
peacefully in Austria's
alpine splendour, the
team journeyed
across the border to
the moody
Hockenheimring in a
German pine forest,
then zig-zagged back
across the map to the
Hungaroring, which
twists around the hills
outside Budapest.

"In the past, my business kept me in the background.

Formula One racing is popular in over 200 countries, including China, where a Grand Prix will be held in the new millennium. A media contingent from China asked Craig what to expect.

Now, it's part of my job to be in the public eye and represent the team."

CRAIG POLLOCK

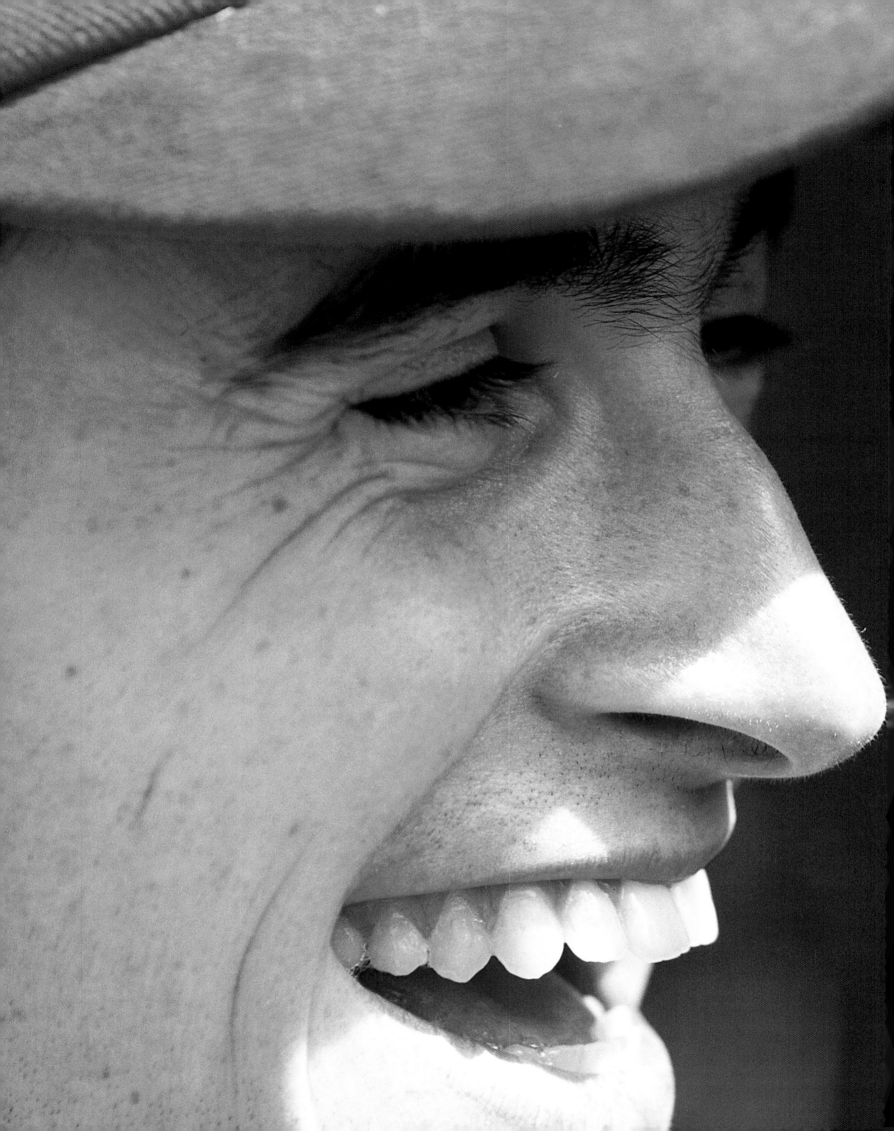

smiling in the face of adversity...

Ricardo's weekend in Germany was not a happy one, yet he was always a happy team player. In practice on Friday, his car had a hydraulic leak, then an engine failure. On Saturday morning, his running time was restricted by a clutch problem. On both days, his mechanics worked overtime to get him back into action, and Ricardo praised them for it. In qualifying, Jacques thanked Ricardo for towing him down the Hockenheimring's long straights to improve his time. In the race, Jacques crashed on the first lap and Ricardo retired later with an engine failure, but he did not look unhappy. "I try to keep a smile all the time," Ricardo says, "and have a good relationship with all the team. In this way, you give motivation to everybody and they give it back to you. It was hard for a while to smile after my injury, the worst of my career. But I was happy to come back and still be able to help the team."

"Ricardo has tremendous talent as a driver. From the team point of view, he is a real gentleman and a pleasure to deal with. He's a great representative for the sport." – Tom Moser

SPA - BELGIUM

a strong comeback from a staggering setback...

The magnificent Spa-Francorchamps circuit, in the Ardennes forest of south-eastern Belgium, is the greatest road racing circuit in the world. The daunting roller-coaster ride of a track is also one of the most dangerous, and when both Jacques and Ricardo became victims of its many pitfalls, the team was put to the sternest possible test. In qualifying, within moments of each other and at the same notoriously difficult Eau Rouge corner, Jacques and Ricardo suffered huge accidents. Mercifully, they were unhurt, thanks to the strength of the BAR chassis, but both cars were completely destroyed. Gathering together their strength and stamina, the team members worked non-stop through Saturday night and were rewarded on Sunday when Jacques' rebuilt car made it to the chequered flag, giving him his first race finish for the team. "There is no such word as 'can't' for us," according to Simon Wachter, the team's Spares Co-Ordinator. "We can do anything. It's just a question of how we do it and how long it will take."

Working throughout Saturday night in the garage at Spa, the team salvaged components from the wreckage and combined them with two test cars re-routed from a scheduled test in Italy. By daylight Sunday morning, two race cars and a spare were ready for action.

upward mobility among the *tifosi*...

The Autodromo Nazionale di Monza, a hallowed shrine of speed for Formula One racing, is the home of the *tifosi* – the fanatical Ferrari fans. Since Gilles Villeneuve remains the most popular Ferrari driver in the Italian team's lengthy history, his son Jacques is always welcome at Monza. Jacques knows the circuit well, having raced there at the beginning of his career in saloons and in Formula 3. His team-mate Ricardo says, "Monza is a beautiful circuit with all the overhanging trees and the parts of the historic old track that are still there. There is always a great atmosphere and the Italian fans are just so enthusiastic about racing." A wheel-bearing problem prevented Ricardo from finishing, but there were *tifosi* cheers for Jacques when he crossed the finish line in eighth place, his best result so far.

While Italian racing red is naturally favoured by the highly partisan *tifosi*, Ricardo thrust the British American Racing colours into the action at Monza.

●●● "What we want to achieve is a level of success, as individuals and as a team, that is commensurate with a professional organisation. Our goal for the millennium is to have those achievements recognised and supported by what we hope is a large following of fans around the world, who will say that these are good people doing a good job."

TOM MOSER

Suzanne Meldrum, Head of Sponsorship Communications for British American Tobacco, closely follows the team's performance. The dividends at Monza included an eighth-place finish for Jacques, his best result for British American Racing. No matter where he finishes, little Jessica Villeneuve is proud of her big brother Jacques.

From the boardroom
at Brackley, Ian Ross,
the team's Chief
Operating Officer,
visits the garage where
Chief Mechanic
Alastair Gibson
(bottom) presides
over preparation of
the car awaited by the
stars of the 'Jacques
and Jock Show.'

"You
can have all the right
technology, all the right machin-
ery, the best of everything, but unless
you have the right people it means noth-
ing in racing. I firmly believe we have
the right people here in this team. They
are our bottom line – our greatest
asset for the future of our
organisation."

RICK GORNE ● ● ●